Voice Of Shades

Nishi Shrama

Made with ❤ on the BookLeaf Publishing Platform
www.bookleafpub.in
www.bookleafpub.com

Dedication

To my parents, who always knew I had something to say, and always encouraged me to express my feelings in words. To my sister, who's been my biggest cheerleader from the start. To my husband, who not only supports my poetry but also tolerates the endless 'poet mood' moments, late-night writing marathons, and my 'this poem is genius!' rants. To my son who has filled my life with joy ,love and inspirations. And to my dear friend, the secret editor, who fixed my words when I thought they were perfect. This book is a little bit of all of you—thank you for making this dream possible with your love, patience, and laughter.

Preface

This collection of poems is not just a book; Voice of shades is a journey through my thoughts, emotions, and experiences. Writing has always been my way of making sense of the world, of capturing fleeting moments and transforming them into something tangible. Poetry has allowed me to speak when words felt too heavy or when silence was all I could offer.

The poems in this book are a reflection of the people who've shaped my life—the ones who have been my pillars of support, laughter, and inspiration. It is because of their love, encouragement, and sometimes their patience (especially my husband's!) that I was able to bring this collection to life.

This book is my gift to you, but it's also a piece of my heart. I hope these poems resonate with you as they have with me, and that you find within them a little bit of yourself.

With love and gratitude,
Nishi Sharma

Acknowledgements

As a psychologist, I've had the privilege of witnessing the full spectrum of human emotions and experiences. This unique perspective has deeply influenced my poetry, allowing me to explore the complexities of the heart and mind. Each poem in this collection reflects not only my own journey but the shared stories and emotions I've encountered along the way.

To my family—my parents, husband, son and sister—thank you for your unwavering support and belief in me. Your encouragement has been a constant source of inspiration.

I'm also deeply grateful to my dear friend for their wisdom and perspective, which have shaped this work in profound ways.

Finally, to the readers of this book, thank you for engaging with these words. This collection is as much yours as it is mine.

With gratitude,
Nishi Sharma

1. Limitless

Within a tiny mind, a universe resides,
A symphony of talents, where dreams abide.
When it dares to soar, to break its chain,
The world unfolds—vast and unrestrained.

No walls can bind, no chains can tie,
It needs no hand, no nod, no guide.
For its wings are strong, its spirit free,
The sky alone its destiny.

It learns, it grows, it finds its way,
Through darkest nights and brightest day.
With hope to lead, it will not fall,
It rises up, above it all.

The heart that dares to dream so wide,
Knows nothing can turn the tide.
For within, it holds the power,
To bloom and grow, to rise and tower.

No fear, no doubt can hold it down,
For in its strength, it wears a crown.
So let it soar, let it be bold,
For within, it has a world to hold.

The future's wide, it's all its own,
A world of dreams, where it has grown.
With every step, it's on its way,
To shape the world, to light the day.

-Nishi Sharma

2. What will they say??

What will they say??
The four words
More powerful than the swords
The four words
More attached than the chords
Words we hear
Every Time we spread out our wings
Words played more
Than the craziest guitar strings
Are you blithe
How can you be?
Oh! Feeling Quixotic..
Aren't you afraid??
"What will they say"
No matter, how inveighed you are..
Courage is still so far
No no! Don't talk about the problems in your marriage..
Better talk about the cars in your garage...
Nor about the passion during your first kiss...
The first meeting and the bliss..

" What will they say"
Never about the dreams you have,
They have a criteria..
You are not enough brave,
They attack like bacteria..
We belong to the middle class..
They have power like stone..
And our pride is like a glass..
Ah ha! Don't look for the diamond,
Be happy with the clay..
" What will they say"
Don't talk about the grief during the death..
Excitement of your baby's breath..
Don't talk about the pain or the tear..
Success or the cheer..
Pain during the labour ..
Shh! They might be your neighbour...
" What will they say"
Ohh! You are so fat...
Don't wear that hat..
Your complexion is not good...
Hey don't eat that food..
The day is not so far..
When you ll be warned,
Don't dare to breath
"what will they say"
These words are more powerful than any religion and

dream..
More sticky than the cream..
More intense than the emotions..
Isn't just a notion...
It arises everywhere..
It must be a poisonous hay..
"What will they say"

-Nishi Sharma

4. Thoughts

In my behemoth mind...

a thing,

like nothing,

may be a cloud

shouting out loud

body pale and pine

and dark as a wine.

Something so old

yet too bold.

Something so bright, but little tired.

Popping up, popping up

and never getting retired.

Have worries about tomorrow,

things I wanna borrow,

lots of emotions...

Laws of motion???

Something about lost glove,

something inspired by love...

Ohh that's just a notion!!

Some lost in hate,

few developed by faith.

Thing that let me drown,

maybe that's frown.

Something about the beautiful world,

motivated by a word,

about what I have learn

and what life has taught...

Okay! Okay!

Let's talk about our thoughts.....

Nishi Sharma

3. Eternal

The moments that we have shared were yours, were
mine,
The moments yet to come, staring through the door of
time.
The paths cross and diverge,
The paths we choose hold hours of charm, certainty,
Peace, simplicity, grace.
Perhaps someday, they may lose their place.

But if you ever feel alone, or think I am gone,
The time that will come may conceal our love,
or distances can apart us.
Then keep alive the hollow nights we spent alone,
The mornings we've missed,
Commemorate that touch, the time we kissed.

Take my life, take my pain,
The sunshine and the rain.
Take my past, and the blame for my sin,

Give me your sky, give me your wings.
Your weakness, your strength, your loss,
Make me win.

Stay strong, stay bold,
I am here, waiting for you—don't you fear.
With the hope to see you soon,
I've passed the sun and the moon.

Nishi Sharma

5. She is the HOME

I've often heard, they say a woman has no home,
That she's always searching, forever to roam.
But I've found, she is the home, in every way,
In her heart, the warmth of the world will stay.

When she becomes a mother, she is the place,
A mother's love, a tender, sacred space.
Her arms, a haven, her heart, a shore,
Her home is in the love she gives, and more.

Then comes the grandmother's embrace so kind,
A place where memories and love unwind.
Her wisdom, her laughter, the stories she shares,
A home in her presence, beyond compare.

When her lover returns, weary and torn,
She is his home, where love is reborn.
Her embrace is a refuge, her soul his guide,
In her, he finds peace, with nowhere to hide.

She heals his spirit, so gentle and pure,
In her arms, his heart is reassured.
A woman's love, a shelter so true,
Where all his burdens fade, and strength renews.

And when the world leaves her tired and worn,
She returns to herself, where strength is reborn.
Her home is within her, calm and serene,
A place where her soul is always seen.

So though they say a woman has no place,
She is the home, full of love and grace.
In every role, in every stride,
A woman's heart is where love will reside.

-Nishi Sharma

6. MAY BE! this is love

Whenever I ask which color fits me right,
He gifts me both, with love shining bright.
If I get angry, he calms me with care,
With something sweet, a tender affair.

He teases and argues over every small thing,
But when I'm upset, like a child, he'll sing.
When I dance to my favorite tune,
He watches, lost, beneath the moon.

Then softly, he whispers, eyes full of grace,
"Stay happy forever, in my warm embrace."
Whatever I do, he boasts with pride,
Telling the world how lucky he is to have me by his
side.

He cherishes every little thing I do,
In my beauty, in my soul, his love feels so true.
Maybe this is love, simple and pure,
A bond that's eternal, a feeling so sure.

Nishi Sharma

7. Perpetrators

These aspirations..
Running in the veins,
Passed through generation to generation..

These attempts to prevail the insanity,
conversations of profanity..

Lands barren, oceans flooded,
Hearts parched and thoughts blooded..

shoving each other down,
In the heat of clown..

Conifers are for museums, Creatures for experiments,
Love for objects And emotions belligerent...

This world we have concocted full of desires
and vanity, too coy and engaged
to live in pursuits of love,
aren't we the perpetrators of humanity????

-Nishi Sharma

16

8. Let them unfold

They will rise once more,
The voices that were lost before,
They will rise with strength anew,
The dreams we've kept, the hopes we knew.
Let's give them life, let them take flight,
The burdens we've hidden in the night.

Some farewells that weighed us down,
Some joys we saved, we'll now unbound,
Let's set them free, let them ignite,
The desires we've kept out of sight.

The vision of a world we've seen,
The journey of peace, forever serene,
The hopes, the dreams, the fire we seek,
The love that makes our spirits speak.
Let's bring them forth, let them unfold,
The prayers we've whispered, quiet yet bold.

Nishi Sharma

9. Words

You had complaints, from my gifts of rhyme,
But what can a poet give, in such fleeting time?
The heart yearns for freedom, the body must fade,
Yet it's these words that eternal truth have made.

Words that can never capture, the moments we've known,
But they reflect every memory we've ever sown.
This is the language of the world we see,
The essence of life in its raw decree.

These words are my soul, my deepest plea,
They are Meera, they are Mohan, they set me free.
Hope and faith, they bloom and grow,
In every verse, in every flow.

Though we may not walk side by side,
The tales of your love in my words abide.
The comfort of your touch, the peace I find,
Woven in verses, eternally entwined.

They will remain, through every phase,
In every moment, through all the days.
This is the power, the gift of the word,
An eternal echo, forever heard.

-Nishi Sharma

10. A heart left Behind

Who knows what sorrow took its hold,
Fate carved by lines so cruel and bold,
Neither victory gained, nor defeat to claim,
Yet joy came quietly, without a name.
What I couldn't keep, fate wouldn't allow,
It gave no chance to hold it now.

I breathed with hope, though weak and slow,
Inching forward, though I didn't know,
I couldn't stop, nor could I wait,
The road ahead was sealed by fate.
One morning, the moon so cold,
Shined like the sun, a sight untold,
A light that never touched the night,
But left the world in half-lit fright.

I wrote it often on pages torn,
A friend, a lover, a love forlorn,
That lover, too, with a tender air,
Left me with nothing, just silent despair.

Neither health nor sickness did I find,
Only a peace, a heart left blind.

-Nishi Sharma

11. Breath

When you're tired, take a deep breath,
Hold yourself gently, with love and rest.
When your heart and mind are at war,
Pause for a moment, breathe deep once more.

When fear holds you back from moving ahead,
When darkness seems to cover the path you tread,
When the light feels distant, out of sight,
Take a deep breath, and hold yourself tight.

This breath will remind you of your place,
In this vast world, with its endless space,
It will whisper softly that you belong,
A vital part of this universe, ever strong.

When you need to reconnect with your soul,
And time seems to weigh heavy, taking its toll,
That deep breath will remind you, you see,
You're an essential piece of eternity.

At every turn where you feel lost,
That breath will guide you, no matter the cost,
You'll rediscover who you are,
For you are a star, born from the dark.

-Nishi Sharma

12. Reunion

The moments that we have shared were yours, were
mine,
The moments yet to come, staring through the door of
time.
The paths cross and diverge,
The paths we choose hold hours of charm, certainty,
Peace, simplicity, grace.
Perhaps someday, they may lose their place.

But if you ever feel alone, or think I am gone,
The time that will come may conceal our love,
or distances can part us.
Then keep alive the hollow nights we spent alone,
The mornings we've missed,
Commemorate that touch, the time we kissed.

Take my life, take my pain,
The sunshine and the rain.
Take my past, and the blame for my sin,
Give me your sky, give me your wings.

Your weakness, your strength, your loss,
Make me win.

Stay strong, stay bold,
I am here, waiting for you—don't you fear.
With the hope to see you soon,
I've passed the sun and the moon.

-Nishi Sharma

13. Echo of love

And love—oh love—such twisted ties,
It lifts us up, then leaves us wise.
A promise broken, lost in time,
A song that once felt so sublime.

We held it close, this fragile dream,
But love slipped through like silent steam.
The words we spoke now fade away,
Like echoes lost at the end of the day.

We hold onto things we cannot keep,
Fading whispers, secrets too deep.
A heart once whole, now torn apart,
Left with pieces, a shattered heart.

We cry for dreams that never wake,
For paths we've lost, for love's mistake.
What once was bright now turns to night,
Chasing shadows, lost from sight.

Every corner holds a ghost,
Of what we loved, of what we've lost the most.
The heart still beats, but feels no flame,
A hollow rhythm, a broken name.

And still, we search through endless tears,
Hoping for love, but drowning in fears.
For now, we wander, cold and alone,
With the echo of love, a heart overthrown.

-Nishi Sharma

14. Emotions

Beneath the surface, whispers rise,
Silent storms that fill our eyes.
A quiet war we fight within,
Where joy and sorrow both begin.

Lust and longing, a fleeting dance,
An urge, a pull, a stolen glance.
But when the fire starts to fade,
Only ashes are left to trade.

Regret seeps in, a heavy cloak,
A past we cannot yet revoke.
It clings to skin, a constant weight,
A reminder of what we can't erase.

Anger bubbles, sharp and bright,
A blaze that burns, a fire's bite.
But once it's spent, what's left to find?
Empty echoes, peace behind.

And love—oh love—what tangled thread,
It lifts us up, then leaves us dead.
A promise made, then lost in time,
A song once sweet, now out of rhyme.

We hold onto what we cannot keep,
And cry for things we cannot speak.
Yet through the cracks, we still seek light,
Chasing shadows in the night.

Each emotion, a quiet thief,
Stealing parts of us, in brief.
But in the end, we are still whole,
Carried forward by the soul.

For even when the world feels cold,
The heart still beats, the truth unfolds—
That we, though bruised, are not undone,
We carry on, until the sun.

-Nishi Sharma

15. Unstoppable

Why fear the ocean when the waves are untamed?
My desires are fierce, unshackled, unclaimed.
Without hesitation, I'll kiss you, O distant goal,
For now, my dreams are naked, they take control.

Every defeat will bloom into a fierce win,
Every shattered heart will rise from within.
No more waiting, no more doubt, no more delay,
My courage is wealth, and I'm here to stay.

Every hope will be counted, every tear turned gold,
For now, my spirit is unbreakable, bold.
The storm may rage, but I'll never fall,
I stand tall, with the world at my call.

-Nishi Sharma

16. It Feels Good!

In a crowd, when someone calls my name,
It feels good, like a fire, igniting the flame.
When the moon rests, and the world is asleep,
It feels good to rise, from the silence so deep.

When all hope slips away, drifting like sand,
It feels good to search, to take back my stand.
When the world feels distant, cold as a stone,
It feels good to find comfort, to know I'm not alone.

In this hidden world, where masks are worn,
It feels good to be me, reborn and transformed.
In a place where I feel lost, and none seem to see,
It feels good to find my worth, simply by being me.

In the chaos, when the world grows loud,
It feels good to stand tall, unshaken, unbowed.
For in the stillness, when I'm left to decide,
It feels good to embrace myself, with love as my guide.

When the weight of the world tries to pull me down,
It feels good to rise, wearing my own crown.
Through every tear, through every fight,
It feels good to know I am my own light.

-Nishi Sharma

17. Culture.. as we know it

Everything is a culture..
Not only music, dance or sculpture.
From dressing to food,
And food to languages,
Saints in cities,
And Sadhu's in villages.
Different provinces and languages sitting under a roof,
Sent that rocket in the universe,
Rainbow be the proof.

Diwali is Lakshmi,
Pongal is cultivation,
Garba is pooja,
And bhangra is a tradition.
Rivers are holy,
And cricket is a religion.
From the fields of green
to the skies up high,
Every place is different,
but we still stand by.

In the morning's light, or the night so bright,
Culture is in us, every day, every night.

The stories of old,
the songs we sing,
We carry them forward,
like a precious ring.
In every street,
there's laughter to hear,
History lives on, far and near.
The prayers we say,
the songs we sing,
Culture is life, it's everything.

Kerala's wisdom,
the culture of books,
And every tradition in every nook.
Temple, Church, Gurudwara or Durgah,
Ishwar for some
and some call him Allah.
Some may stand and some may sit...
Culture... as we know it!

-Nishi Sharma

18. Two Pillars.

Two pillars strong, side by side,
A bond that time can never divide.
One stands tall with quiet grace,
The other's warmth, a soft embrace.

Each has a role, both distinct and clear,
Yet together, they conquer every fear.
One's love is fierce, a guiding light,
The other's gentle, soft as night.

Through sleepless nights and endless days,
They carve out paths in countless ways.
Different hearts, yet shared in rhyme,
Two souls aligned through endless time.

One lifts you up with steady hands,
The other dreams with future plans.
Yet both, in silence or in song,
Build the strength where you belong.

From your first breath, they took their place,
Pillars of love, an endless space.
Together they stand, through joy and tears,
A steadfast bond that conquers years.

For their love may differ, their roles may shift,
But side by side, they gift you lift.
Two pillars strong, unyielding, true,
Parents forever, just for you.

In laughter's echo and whispered fears,
Their hearts entwined through passing years.
With every challenge, they pave the way,
Planting bright seeds for you to sway.

When shadows loom and doubts arise,
They stand as shields, your sunlit skies.
Each story shared, a thread well-spun,
Two guiding stars, forever one.

-Nishi Sharma

19. Those who keep going.

To the ones who bear the weight,
Carrying burdens none can relate,
With heavy hearts and shoulders worn,
Fighting battles from the day they're born.

To the ones who find it hard to share,
Who hold their pain, but still, they care,
You walk alone but rise again,
Stronger through the silent rain.

To the ones who've felt the ache of night,
In shadows deep, away from light,
You are not forgotten, nor unseen,
You are the warriors in between.

To the ones who've fought, yet still they stand,
With trembling hearts and shaking hands,
Know that every tear you've cried,
Has built a strength you cannot hide.

To the ones who search for love,
A gentle hand, a touch, a hug,
Know that love will find its way,
In your own time, it'll light the day.

To the ones who struggle just to breathe,
Whose dreams are heavy, hearts deceive,
You are amazing, don't you see?
The world's still waiting, just for thee.

So rise, you mighty soul, take flight,
Embrace your path, reclaim your light,
You conquer fear, you break the chain,
The world is yours, through joy or pain.

You are loved, you are enough,
Your journey's hard, but you are tough.
Keep going forward, don't turn back,
For you are the strength you sometimes lack.

-Nishi Sharma

20. Memories

Some make me smile, some make me weep,
Moments I wish I could still keep.
I remember the first time I saw your face,
The warmth, the laughter, your soft embrace.

But time has a way of pulling them apart,
Leaving behind a piece of my heart.
The love I thought would never fade,
Now only echoes in the silence it made.

Then there were friends, who stood by my side,
Through every fall, every tear I tried to hide.
We laughed, we cried, we dreamed so big,
But even the strongest bonds can break, just like a twig.

I remember those college nights,
When the world seemed perfect, full of lights.
We thought we knew it all, we thought we were free,
But life had lessons no one could see.

And failure—oh, how it cuts so deep,
It's the quiet pain I couldn't speak.
The dreams I chased, but never caught,
The battles I fought, but somehow lost.

There was a love I thought would stay,
A love that promised it would never stray.
But promises fade, like sand through hands,
Leaving behind only shifting strands.

The betrayal still stings like a silent scream,
A friendship lost, a shattered dream.
But in the pain, I found my strength,
In letting go, I learned at length.

And then came the days when I was alone,
Wandering a world that felt unknown.
But somehow, somewhere, love found me again,
In the arms of family, and friends who felt like rain.

Through every failure, every tear,
I found that those who truly care,
Were the ones who held me when I fell,
Their love was my shelter, my personal spell.

Success arrived, but in quiet grace,
Not in loud cheers, or a boastful face.

It was the peace in knowing I had tried,
The calm after the storm, when the pain had died.

And now I sit, with all these memories,
Of love, loss, pain, and victories.
The faces may fade, the voices may cease,
But these moments, these memories—they will never
release.

Because they've shaped me, every single part,
Carved deep inside, forever in my heart.
Through the betrayals, the love, the smiles,
It's the memories that make life worthwhile.

-Nishi Sharma

21. Smile

A smile, so soft, yet heavy in its grace,
It hides the storms that time can't erase.
Behind the curve, the laughter may not lie,
But shadows linger in a tear-filled eye.

It whispers hope in a world that turns cold,
A mask for a heart, for a story untold.
With every flash, a secret is kept,
A promise of strength where silence has wept.

It holds the beauty of the sky,
A light that flickers, never to die.
Though life may break and hearts may fall,
A smile can mend the cracks in us all.

Beneath the joy, there's a deep unseen,
A battle fought on the edges between.
For every grin, there's a weight to bear,
A moment of peace in a life unfair.

But still it shines, a beacon in the dark,
A flicker of light, a fleeting spark.
A smile can break through the hardest night,
Even if the soul is lost from sight.

It carries warmth like morning sun,
A promise that the dark is done.
Through every tear, it still can rise,
A fleeting moment that never lies.

A smile can heal what words can't say,
It carries love in the gentlest way.
It's more than joy, it's more than light,
It's the courage to face the longest night.

So smile, for the world will never know
The courage it takes to let the darkness go.
A smile can heal what words cannot find,
A bittersweet remedy for a troubled mind.

-Nishi Sharma

22. I am enough.

I am me.
A little broken, yet stitched with silken threads,
Scattered a thousand times, yet gathered like pearls
again.

I have burned like the first light of dawn,
And drowned in the depths of my own night.
With a single smile, I can light up the world,
With my fragrance, I make the air come alive.

I have wept in silence, heart heavy with storms,
Yet risen, unshaken, to battle them all.
I have been fearless, fire in my veins,
Yet trembled at the weight of a whisper.

A mother, a wife, a daughter—I try,
Yet some days, I wonder—am I enough?
But I am not just a question, I am the answer.
Not just a shadow, I am the light.

I am me. I am you.
I am strength, I am scars, I am survival.
I am fire, I am tenderness, I am truth.
And above all—
I am enough.

-Nishi Sharma

23. Nature

As time unfolds, what we behold,
The peace we seek, the calm we're told,
Becomes our nature, shaped by hands,
While true nature slips through shifting sands.

We crave the forests, rivers deep,
The gardens rich, the mountains steep,
Yet in our hunger, we take away,
And call it progress, day by day.

With dreams and desires, we teach the young,
To reach for stars, to sing, to run,
But in our greed, we pull them far,
Leaving their dreams lost, a distant star.

We carve through forests, drain the streams,
Build on the land that once had dreams,
And then we say, "This is the way,"
As nature's beauty fades away.

We change the course of rivers' flow,
And pave the paths where wild things go,
Forgetting that with every stone,
We rob the earth, we make it lone.

And later, when regret takes hold,
We blame the world, the tales we're told,
Saying this is nature, this is fate,
Yet we, ourselves, have sealed its state.

For greed has shaped what once was pure,
And in its wake, we seek a cure,
But in the end, it's clear to see,
We've shaped this world, and lost its plea.

-Nishi Sharma

24. One day, all grow old

The laughter fades, the joyful sound,
The little feet that ran around,
Now walk away, no longer near,
The innocence lost, the childhood dear.
One day, all grow old.

Your children, once your pride and light,
Now walk their paths, no longer tight.
The joy, the chaos, the endless play,
Now a memory, fading away.
One day, all grow old.

Your life partner, once your closest friend,
Now walks beside you, but near the end.
The love, the passion, once so true,
Now whispers softly, shared by few.
One day, all grow old.

Your parents, once the hands that held,
Now grow frail, their stories quelled.
The wisdom shared, the care they gave,
Now soft as whispers, gentle as a wave.
One day, all grow old.

Your siblings, once your closest kin,
Now live their lives, their own to spin.
The fights, the laughs, the tears once near,
Now fade away, as time draws near.
One day, all grow old.

Your grandparents, who held you high,
Now rest beneath the same old sky.
The stories they told, the love they gave,
Now memories that gently wave.
One day, all grow old.

Your friends, once by your side each day,
Now drift apart, each finds their way.
The late-night talks, the dreams once spun,
Now distant whispers, long undone.

One day, all grow old.

And time takes all, yet leaves behind,
The love we gave, the ties that bind.
In every hug, in every tear,
The moments live, still ever near.
One day, all grow old.

-Nishi Sharma

25. Voice of Shades

In the quiet corners where thoughts collide,
Shadows murmur, voices hide.
Faint whispers drift on the edge of light,
A dance of dark, a breath of night.

Not all that speaks is heard aloud,
Some words are wrapped in a shrouded cloud.
Each shade a story, soft and deep,
A secret meant for waking sleep.

They flicker, blend, then slip away,
The unspoken truths they dare not say.
In every shade, a voice resounds,
Beneath the surface, it surrounds.

The hues of joy, the tints of fear,
Whispered desires, the truths we fear.
Voice of Shades, they echo in the still,
A silent song, a soft-spun thrill.

In shadows cast by the moon's embrace,
Voice of Shades linger, a fleeting grace.
A voice that trembles, faint but clear,
A shade that speaks when none can hear.

-Nishi Sharma